Honesty Power!
Local Directories Work
All You Need to Know

By Oscar Smith

Honesty Power! Local Directories Work All You Need to Know **By Oscar Smith**

© 2016 Oscar Smith. ALL RIGHTS RESERVED. No part of this book may be reproduced or transmitted in any form whatsoever, electronic, or mechanical, including photocopying, recording, or by any informational storage or retrieval system without the expressed written, dated and signed permission from the author.

LIMITS OF LIABILITY / DISCLAIMER OF WARRANTY:

The author and publisher of this book have used their best efforts in preparing this material. The author and publisher make no representation or warranties with respect to the accuracy, applicability, fitness, or completeness of the contents of this program. They disclaim any warranties (expressed or implied), merchantability, or fitness for any particular purpose. The author and publisher shall in no event be held liable for any loss or other damages, including but not limited to special, incidental, consequential, or other damages. As always, the advice of a competent legal, tax, accounting or other professional should be sought.

TABLE OF CONTENTS

About the Author .... **Error! Bookmark not defined.**

What is an online local directory? .... **Error! Bookmark not defined.**

Are online local directories the same as search engines? .... **Error! Bookmark not defined.**

Why is it important that my business be listed in an online local directory? 5

Can small businesses profit from using online local directories? 6

Is it difficult to sign up to an online local directory? 7

How much do online local directories cost? 8

Is it worth paying money to be listed in a local online directory, when so many of them are available for free? 9

What are the best online local directories to use? 10

What is a featured listing? .... **Error! Bookmark not defined.**

What are different types of online local directories? 12

How can I find a niche local online directory? 13

How can online directory listings boost traffic to my website? .. **Error! Bookmark not defined.**

How can online listings help me develop my business' brand image? 15

Will online local directories help me target my business to relevant audiences? 16

Should I use keywords in my listing? 17

What should I include within the description of my listing? 18

What is the difference between citations and links? 19

Should I respond to negative feedback or reviews on online directories that allow them? .... **Error! Bookmark not defined.**

What should I watch out for when checking out online local directories? .... **Error! Bookmark not defined.**

Should I list my business in every online local directory possible? .... **Error! Bookmark not defined.**

Should I keep my username and password the same on all online local directories? .... **Error! Bookmark not defined.**

What if I can't remember if my business is already located in an online local directory? .... **Error! Bookmark not defined.**

Is it necessary to read through *every* directory's Terms of Service? .... **Error! Bookmark not defined.**

Can I hand off the task of listing my business in the many different online local directories? .... **Error! Bookmark not defined.**

Do I need to do anything after my business is listed? .... **Error! Bookmark not defined.**

Next Steps .... **Error! Bookmark not defined.**

ABOUT THE AUTHOR

Oscar Smith, Author and Visionary Thought Leader over 875 worldwide published articles and over 12 books. His compelling, clear and concise way of articulating his insights places Oscar in a unique position as a Marketplace- based Chaplain. His counsel is regularly sought by friends and business associates from around the world. Prayer Power, He Came Incognito, A Word Made Flesh and Gladiator Ali Marketing Genius are his most recent books. Honesty Is Power! Explores the impact oft of new online business directories and social media on every business. Building stronger customer relationships and customer experiences with honesty and trust is the pathway for the future viability for every business. Whenever two people interact – either face to face or online – one of the most important subtexts of that interaction is honesty and trust. If we don't trust each other, any interaction between us just won't be very efficient.

Today, of course, we no longer fear this kind of behavior from businesses (at least, not from "legitimate" businesses). We put our e-mail addresses and mobile phone numbers on our business cards now, and include them in articles and presentations for public consumption, distributing them just as widely as we do our postal addresses or business phone numbers. And companies refrain from abusing this information at least partly because *they would be found out*. Even if there were no regulatory penalty at all, to be found abusing any person's contact details would immediately tarnish a company's reputation.

Customer expectations for complete honesty and trust are rising. Over time, customers will be holding businesses to an entirely new and tougher standard when it comes to watching out for customer interests. Honesty Is Power! Global New Local Business Directories appreciate your support.

It All Starts with Honesty Is Power!

INTRODUCTION

Businesses need exposure on the major directories for many reasons.

- Citations - Site Ranking
- Credibility - Reputation
- Mobile SEO
- And more...

Honesty Power!

Covers Local, National and Global Directories like

Angies List, City Search, FourSquare

Google My Biz - LinkedIn - MapQuest

Merchant Circle - SuperPages – Yelp and more.

This compilation is from several experts from literally around the world in the area of search engine optimization and innovative techniques that will help you plan an effective way to getting listed in Online Directories. Our goal was to offer an array of options from basic to advanced cutting edge ideas.

Take time to visit the book website (http://www.MtJuliet1.com) for FAQs and to post your own burning questions. You'll have access to special offers and discounts on various SEO tools and services. You can also get exclusive access to instructional videos related to the concepts in the book by sending an email to Info@MtJuliet1.com

WHAT IS AN ONLINE LOCAL DIRECTORY?

An online local directory is a website that lists businesses, usually within categories. These directories allow business owners to list their business, get their name in front of the customers, and give customers the information they need to contact the business. It also narrows the World Wide Web down to local communities and places, and makes local businesses more accessible to the customers that use them.

The details provided in an online listing will vary from business to business and from directory to directory. Typical information includes:

- The business name
- Address
- Telephone numbers
- Product or service sold
- Number of employees
- The area the business services
- Professional associations the business belongs to
- Reviews, comments, and feedback (on some sites)

ARE ONLINE LOCAL DIRECTORIES THE SAME AS SEARCH ENGINES?

Online local directories often have a search function within them. This makes it easier for users to quickly find the business they're looking for, without having to search through thousands of listings. However, this does not make these directories search engines.

Search engines can find just about any information you need and provide in-depth articles, pictures, and blog posts about very specific topics. Search engines list the actual URLs to websites and will take you directly to them. Online local directories will provide users with many different results, but each of those results will only be a business listing including very basic information.

Search engines will also pick up on the various web pages within a website, giving each a different page ranking dependent on things such as keywords and traffic numbers. Online local directories on the other hand, will provide only one URL, and it's typically only to the home page of the website.

The way in which local directories and search engines work behind the scenes also distinguish the two. Online directories use people to manually review, proofread and approve each listing. Search engines on the other hand, because they're dealing with so much more information, must rely on highly complex computer-generated indexes that determine which information is displayed.

WHY IS IT IMPORTANT THAT MY BUSINESS BE LISTED IN AN ONLINE LOCAL DIRECTORY?

According to a study conducted by Burke, 8 out of 10 shoppers will use an online directory to guide them in the direction of where to go for whatever product or service they are looking for.

Of that group, 8 out of 10 shoppers who used a directory to find what they needed will end up buying something now or in the future from the business they found within the directory.

This is why it's so important to have your business listed in an online directory. If customers are already using online directories, they already have a need for your business or service. And if your business isn't listed in an online directory, the chances are good that the competition will be, and customers will turn to them instead of you.

This is why it's so important to be listed in online local directories – *so customers can find you!*

CAN SMALL BUSINESSES PROFIT FROM USING ONLINE LOCAL DIRECTORIES?

When thinking about using online local directories, many small businesses make the mistake of thinking it only works for *huge* companies. Companies like Costco that have several locations, sometimes within mere miles of each other. However, it's really small businesses that will benefit the most from online directories. Remember that these directories focus on *local* businesses.

The intent is that it will bring customers to actual brick-and-mortar businesses that are located near them, meaning that small businesses have the most to profit from being listed. And if your business isn't listed, there's a good chance that your competitor's is, and that customers will go to them instead of you.

IS IT DIFFICULT TO SIGN UP TO AN ONLINE LOCAL DIRECTORY?

No! Signing up for a local directory usually just takes just a few minutes and is a simple process that includes only filling out some basic information about your company, then verifying that information via text, email, or phone.

Because business owners are often best served by registering with multiple online local directories, it can take some time, but it's not difficult at all.

HOW MUCH DO ONLINE LOCAL DIRECTORIES COST?

This will vary depending on the directory that you're using. Many of them are free, but there are others that will provide you with more than just a basic listing and typically these directories will charge a larger fee for doing so.

Many online local directories will also provide a basic listing for free, but will give you the option of upgrading to a premium account that will give you more features and options.

IS IT WORTH PAYING MONEY TO BE LISTED IN A LOCAL ONLINE DIRECTORY, WHEN SO MANY OF THEM ARE AVAILABLE FOR FREE?

Marketing consultants often advise that businesses choose one or two of the paid directories (or premium packages) and use those as part of their online marketing. When doing so, it's important that business owners do some research and make sure that they'll see a return on the cost paid to use the site.

You need to make sure that the site is highly reputable and established and, if your better-rated competition is listed on the site, you should be as well. Confining yourself to free listings won't cost you a thing, but it can mean you're missing out on opportunities that in the end, would have multiplied your small initial investment.

WHAT ARE THE BEST ONLINE LOCAL DIRECTORIES TO USE?

There are hundreds of online local directories, but your best bet is to find quality sites that will boost your page ranking and get your business in front of the eyes of the most customers. The top 15 online local directories are:

- Google My Business
- Aabaco Local Listings/LocalWorks (formerly Yahoo)
- Bing Places
- Yelp
- MerchantCircle
- YellowPages.com
- SuperPages.com
- CitySearch
- Mapquest/Yext
- Local.com
- Foursquare
- LinkedIn
- Angie'sList
- CitySlick
- Kudzu

WHAT IS A FEATURED LISTING?

Featured listings are available on some sites for business owners that want their listing to appear higher in the search results. These listings also provide more information about the listing or the business than a basic listing will.

Featured listings do have a higher chance of being clicked on by the user, but they also come with an added fee and so, business owners should make an effort to track these listings specifically to determine whether or not they're worth the added cost.

WHAT ARE THE DIFFERENT TYPES OF ONLINE LOCAL DIRECTORIES?

At first it may seem as though all online local directories are the same, but truthfully there are four different types.

- Data-aggregators. These are directories that gather information and display it in a summary form. These directories are often based on categories and let users see results based on things such as what type of product or service they're looking for. NeustarLocalEze is a good example of a data-aggregator directory. This site allows users to base their search on small businesses, chains and enterprises, or resellers and agencies.

- Horizontal directories. These are directories that don't focus on a specific industry, but instead targets people in many different industries, and the general public. Yelp is a good example of a horizontal directory because it includes businesses of many different industries and is meant for the general public.

- Niche directories. The opposite of horizontal directories, niche directories do target specific industries. It's advisable that you list your business in at least one or two niche directories to further target your audience, stay ahead of the competition, and get the biggest ROI from online directories. Avvo is an example of a niche directory.

- Region-specific directories. These are online directories that focus on one particular area or region, such as http://nybizlist.com/.

HOW CAN I FIND A NICHE LOCAL ONLINE DIRECTORY?

General online directories such as the Yellow Pages or Google My Business are easy to find because just about everybody knows about them. Even if you haven't, a quick search for "online local directories" will quickly give you the results you're looking for.

Online local directories that deal in particular niches however, can seem like they're a bit more challenging to find. The good news is, they aren't.

Start by searching for your keywords, but adding "directory" at the end. So if you're a florist, you can search "florist directory" to find results. If one keyword doesn't provide you with what you're looking for, use another and another until you find the directory you think might be right for your business.

Remember that just like any other online directory, finding it isn't good enough. You'll have to investigate the site a little bit, and make sure that it works for you, and your business.

HOW CAN ONLINE DIRECTORY LISTINGS BOOST TRAFFIC TO MY WEBSITE?

Whenever your business, company, or company URL is listed on website, it helps boost your page ranking. And when that information is listed on an authoritative and established page such as Google My Business or Yellow Pages, Google uses that as an indicator that your website is also established and authoritative.

When you have your website URL listed on several of these authoritative websites, it has several different "votes" in the eyes of Google and the search engines. The more you have, the higher your website URL will appear within the search engine results.

Have enough and your website will even start to appear on the first page of search engine results, sending more and more traffic to your website.

HOW CAN ONLINE LISTINGS HELP ME DEVELOP MY BUSINESS' BRAND IMAGE?

When people think of online local directories, they often think of several typed lines of text indicating the business' name, address, phone number, region serviced, and types of products or services sold. This is largely true, so how is a bunch of typed text going to help you develop your business' brand image?

Easily. When you create a listing on an online local directory, you do more than just input your business' contact information. Typically these sites always ask for a profile picture, which can be your business' logo, which will help develop your brand image. Several sites also have separate sections for things such as photos and videos where you can upload commercials, YouTube videos about your products or services, and even just pictures from company events.

All of this will show your business through images that users will remember more easily, and they help develop your brand image.

WILL ONLINE LOCAL DIRECTORIES HELP ME TARGET MY BUSINESS TO RELEVANT AUDIENCES?

Yes! In fact, that's one of the biggest benefits of using online local directories for your business! When users search for your business using an online local directory, they already need something that you can provide them with – they just need help getting to you.

For instance, you're a small business providing used baby and children clothing to the people in a small town in Texas. You list your business in an online local directory such as YellowPages.com. When people visit this online directory, they search for keywords such as "baby clothing," "children's clothing," or "used clothing." After they perform this search, your business will appear along with others (or not, if your competitors haven't yet discovered the magic of online local business directories!) Once they find your listing, they either then visit the website to purchase the product or get more information, or they visit your store in person.

Targeting your business to relevant audiences is one of the biggest benefits your business will reap from online local directories, and one of the biggest reasons why you need to be listed in them.

SHOULD I USE KEYWORDS IN MY LISTING?

Yes! Remember that the listings you're creating in various online local directories are a form of advertising. And any type of online advertising is dependent on the appropriate use of keywords.

You'll have to be careful when using them, however. Some sites have designated sections within the registration forms for keywords, and they don't want you to use them in other areas of the form or listing. Also remember that the directories are local, meaning that you want keywords that include your location.

WHAT SHOULD I INCLUDE WITHIN THE DESCRIPTION OF MY LISTING?

Just as using the right keywords for your business is important, having the right description is crucial. This is essentially the body of the listing and will let customers and users connect with you and get a better sense of you and your business.

Remember that descriptions have to be short (most local online directories have a cap around 200 characters,) and that they should be memorable. Include tag lines, slogans, and anything else that might stick in the mind of customers when it comes to buying your product or service.

WHAT IS THE DIFFERENCE BETWEEN CITATIONS AND LINKS?

At this stage of the game, it's pretty obvious when you see a link to a website. It typically includes a URL address or a name, is underlined, and is clickable, meaning that clicking on it will take you to a different page or website.

Citations on the other hand, are just mentions of your business. They mean that people are talking about your business, and that's exactly what the search engines look for when calculating page rankings. It's for this reason that citations are often considered to be more valuable than links. However, it's important to know that not all local directories will allow citations.

Directories such as the Yellow Pages merely list the business' information, while directories such as Trip Advisor and Facebook Pages allow interaction with the users and customers through reviews and comments.

You should always make sure that, along with listings-only directories, you're also using directories that allow for citations and that direct interaction with your customers.

SHOULD I RESPOND TO NEGATIVE FEEDBACK OR REVIEWS ON ONLINE DIRECTORIES THAT ALLOW THEM?

The temptation to defend your business from an online review can be great, but it's best that you don't respond directly to the critique. This can often only result in an online shouting match where neither side ever comes out victorious.

But you also can't have negative information out there about your business, especially if it's false. Instead of responding to the review directly, instead contact the directory itself and explain the situation. Point out the errors of the initial comment or review, and allow the site to handle it in a professional manner.

WHAT SHOULD I WATCH OUT FOR WHEN CHECKING OUT ONLINE LOCAL DIRECTORIES?

There are hundreds of online local directories on the web today and just like anything else, there are good directories and there are bad directories. The chances are good that you'll be looking at many directories when it's time to list your business online, so here are some things to watch out for when doing so:

- Free listings not offered. Any reputable online local directory will at least have the option to list your business for free, even if this gives you only a very basic listing. If a directory doesn't at least give you this option, there are plenty of great directories out there that will so you're better off finding and using one of them.

- Low page ranking. Remember that one of the biggest benefits of using online local directories is that they should boost your online brand and presence simply because you're listed on them. If the directory has a low page ranking, being listed on it isn't going to help your own ranking. Instead find an online directory with a high page ranking (there are lots!) to list your business.

- Toxic links. Some online directories are simply set up with the intention of being a feed for backlinks. When this is done too often on one site, Google actually frowns on the practice and will lower the site's ranking even further. Find out how links are being used, and how many are given to any particular listing to determine if the links are being used more as spam than anything else.

- Forced backlinks. This goes along with the above but in

this scenario, the online directory actually requires businesses to have a backlink to the directory placed on the business' website. Truthfully these online directories are only looking to increase their own exposure, and they might not do too much for your business. Use directories that give you the option to place a link onto your website, but that certainly don't require that you do so.

SHOULD I LIST MY BUSINESS IN EVERY ONLINE LOCAL DIRECTORY POSSIBLE?

There are a number of directories out there, and it might seem that because these pages can increase your web traffic and get your name in front of the customers, you should appear on as many as possible. However, this isn't true.

When you start to appear on every directory and have listings everywhere, it can start to seem like spam, and customers and the search engines will start to get tired. Instead, focus on quality directories and, if there are directories specifically for your niche, get listed on those first.

It's also a good idea to implement tracking devices such as unique phone numbers or URLs, to see which directories are giving you the biggest ROI. You can them remove your listing from the directories that aren't doing anything for your website or your business, and try another directory that might give you a bigger profit in the end.

SHOULD I KEEP MY USERNAME AND PASSWORD THE SAME ON ALL ONLINE LOCAL DIRECTORIES?

The chances are good that your username will be the same across all sites, because it will either be your business' name or something related to your business. However, it's best not to use the same password for all sites.

Changing your passwords for various sites will make it harder to hack into them because hackers will need more than just one password. But you also don't want to forget the passwords simply because there are so many different ones to remember.

Use a tracking system, such as Google Drive, for all of your passwords, where they'll be stored securely but will be available for you when you need them. While keeping track of passwords, also keep track of all your login info for each site including your username and the URL of the site and your listing.

WHAT IF I CAN'T REMEMBER IF MY BUSINESS IS ALREADY LOCATED IN AN ONLINE LOCAL DIRECTORY?

You should never register your business with an online local directory without thoroughly checking to make sure your business isn't already listed. It's much easier than business owners think to end up with duplicate listings, and these will be very negative for your site and your business.

They'll confuse and frustrate customers, and they'll add up to lost potential revenue for your business. Duplicate listings can even go against a site's terms of service, which could potentially get you banned from the site, leaving you in the dust of your competition.

Before signing up for any local directory, search everything you can about your business on that site, including the name, phone number, fax number, email addresses, and anything else you can think of. If after searching all of these you still don't come up with any results for your business, go ahead and claim it. However, if you do get results but they're incomplete or inaccurate, make sure you fix the mistakes right away.

IS IT NECESSARY TO READ THROUGH EVERY DIRECTORY'S TERMS OF SERVICE?

It is tempting to simply just check the box that says, "I have read and agree to the Terms of Service for thisonlinedirectory.com, especially when you're creating multiple listings in many different directories. However, this is a mistake.

It's crucial that you read through each site's TOS, as these are the rules of the site and they're often strictly enforced. If you find certain rules that you think are particularly relevant to your business or your listing, such as not having more than one URL displayed, make note of it for your own reference later. Should you break the rules, intentionally or unintentionally, you could be banned from the site, and customers won't be able to find you as very easy.

CAN I HAND OFF THE TASK OF LISTING MY BUSINESS IN THE MANY DIFFERENT ONLINE LOCAL DIRECTORIES?

There are hundreds if not thousands of different online local directories. Signing up for all of them and going through the registration process again and again can take an immense amount of time – time that busy business owners usually don't have.

The good news is that online marketing consultants specialize in doing things just this, they do it every day. They'll be able to get your business listed quicker, and they'll likely already be familiar with the terms of all the major directories.

When hiring an online marketing consultant to take over this task for you, it's important to know that you will still be needed for parts of the process. There are many sites such as LocalEze, YP, and ExpressUpdate, that require verification by phone and a consultant will not be able to do this for you. The directory wants to make sure that they're dealing with you – the authorized owner of the business – and nobody else.

DO I NEED TO DO ANYTHING AFTER MY BUSINESS IS LISTED?

So you've found all the directories you want to be listed in, are signed up and verified, and your business listing is now viewable across multiple sites. There's nothing left for you to do, right?

Wrong! It's important to continually manage and edit your business listings to keep them as accurate as possible. As your business grows, the information might change, or information may just become inaccurate over time. Having a listing with the wrong information is worse than not having a listing at all because it can cause users and customers to become frustrated and turned off of your business.

It's imperative that you or your marketing consultant is constantly managing listings to ensure that they are correct and up to date.

Honesty Power! Local Directories Work All You Need to Know **By Oscar Smith**

PART TWO
SNAPCHAT

WHY SNAPCHAT MARKETING?

If you want to be in business for the long run and stay relevant, you are going to need to keep tabs on the social media landscape and join social networks that are going to take you into the future. That's exactly what Snapchat does. This platform is one of the social media outlets that have come from a constantly evolving world of social media and it uses a novel and never-before-seen method of communicating – a way of communicating that shows where the future of social media is headed.

SNAPCHAT IS ALL ABOUT THE NEXT GENERATION

Do you want one really great reason to join Snapchat? There are way more than one but if you need just one, think about the fact that Snapchat has become one of the most popular social media applications for people aged 12 to 24 years old. As you can see, that means that the next generation of buyers and the generation after that are all going to be potential Snapchat veterans and if your brand is on Snapchat and has been from the beginning, there is a good chance that you're reaching a lot of these young people.

SNAPCHAT CREATES EXCITEMENT

Another great reason to join is that the way that Snapchat works is extremely fun and promotes serious interactivity between users. Snapchat is an exciting way to use social media and brands are capitalizing on these young people's desire for exciting content by providing them with things like behind-the-scenes information about an event or brand, special promotions, discounts or giveaways that they couldn't find out about from any other source. Because of the way that information is communicated and how quickly it disappears, Snapchat promotes excitement with every single post.

SNAPCHAT CAN INCREASE YOUR ONLINE PRESENCE AND GAIN YOU NEW FOLLOWERS

Snapchat is also a great way to increase your online presence. You may already have profiles on websites like Twitter and Facebook, and you probably have a Pinterest account and other social media as well. But whenever you join a major social media network you're going to be expanding your online presence and you will gain followers all around as a result, as well as retain followers better on your other social media networks. In fact, you will have a significant number of people coming to follow you on Snapchat from your other social media profiles as well as having people find that your Twitter and Facebook because they followed you on Snapchat.

No matter how you slice it, Snapchat is one very possible future of social media. Making sure that you are prepared for the next generation of buyers is something that every business should be doing and when you see a social media platform like Snapchat that is gaining popularity so fast – to the tune of 200 million active users per month – you need to get involved as quickly as possible and start using it to build your business even bigger.

CHAPTER ONE:

WHAT EXACTLY IS SNAPCHAT?

Snapchat is a very powerful social media platform that has become very popular as of late. Major brands are not only starting to get their presence onto Snapchat but also advertise on the platform through Snapchat's discovery system. Snapchat is similar to other social media applications in that you create a profile and then have followers or fans that you communicate with. However, that is pretty much the extent of the similarities. Snapchat is remarkably different in the way that users communicate with each other and in the ways that information is shared.

HOW SNAPCHAT WORKS

Snapchat is a program that works with a very specific media for communicating with other users. There are a couple of differences that make this program unique and one of the most interesting social media platforms in use today like using photos and videos to communicate with other people. While Twitter, Facebook and most social media platforms mainly communicate with text, the only text that you will find here is the captions on pictures and videos. Another difference was Snapchat is that when you post your pictures and videos they will only last from 1 to 10 seconds with just a single exception, which we'll get into later.

It might be difficult to understand how this works if you've never used the application. Just imagine that someone you are following on social media posts something and you get an alert. You go to their feed and check what they have posted and it is either a picture with a caption or a short video, or if you didn't get there fast enough, you missed out. That's basically how Snapchat works and you have followers and friends on the platform just like you do with other social media websites.

WHAT'S THE POINT OF SNAPCHAT?

Snapchat is leading the way into the future of social media. This platform is going to be one of the big ones that will serve the next generation of consumers. The app is already being used by most teenagers and even Facebook has seen the value of Snapchat and offered $3 billion for the company. However, the creators of Snapchat believed in their company enough that they refused Facebook's offer. Facebook has people who analyze a great deal of data in order to predict future trends and if they think Snapchat is valuable then brands should be jumping on as quickly as they can.

So, what's the point of Snapchat? To socialize. To build a following. To communicate with other people who share interests with you or have an emotional investment in what you are posting. On one hand, Snapchat is just a social media platform but on the other hand it may be the application which leads the charge into the future where social media posts will be less text and more pictures and video. Brands like Mashable, National Geographic and Comedy Central as well as several dozen others see enough value in Snapchat to advertise with the application as part of the discovery feature and thousands of others have joined the platform as well. If you have a brand – it should be on Snapchat.

CHAPTER TWO:

GETTING YOUR BRAND ON SNAPCHAT

The first thing that you're going to need to do if you want to reap the benefits of the Snapchat application is get your brand onto the platform. This chapter will explain exactly what you need to do to create your Snapchat account and how to fill out your profile information correctly so that your Snapchat is ready to use and you can start getting followers and marketing your brand in new and interesting ways.

SIGNING UP

Obviously, the first thing that you're going to want to do is download the Snapchat application. You can add this app to either your Android or your iOS device. There is no support for Windows operating systems as of yet or any of the lesser-known ones. Once you have Snapchat downloaded on your phone or mobile device, launch it and you'll be taken to a screen where it will ask you to either sign in or sign up. You are going to sign up with the following information:

EMAIL ADDRESS

You want to use an email address that you actually check. In fact, this may be a good time to use your main email address – or the one for your business. Whatever you do, don't just make one up because you will have to verify your account.

PASSWORD AND DATE OF BIRTH

The next thing that you'll enter is your password and your date of birth. There aren't many restrictions with your password and you should have no problem entering one. Your date of birth is also easy, using the date tool that comes with most mobile devices.

YOUR PHONE NUMBER

The last thing that you'll enter is your phone number. You want to enter your valid mobile number because they are going to send you a verification code that you'll have to enter into the app to use it fully.

VERIFICATION CODE

They're going to send you the verification code but you may not be able to enter it into the app without some help navigating to the right place. Since we are going to get into navigation in a later chapter, and explain where everything is, for now just know that the place you enter your verification code is under the gear icon that opens the settings menu.

YOUR PROFILE AND LOGO

Snapchat doesn't have a place for you to fill out your profile like Twitter and Facebook and other social media platforms do. In fact, you can't even upload your logo from the app. The only thing that you can do if you want to customize your profile picture from the app is take a picture of either your face or a picture of your logo and customize it that way. The problem with this method is that it doesn't look professional and sense Snapchat takes a series of five pictures, quickly in a row to make an animated GIF, it is impossible to hold your hand steady enough to get a decent picture, even if you have a high quality camera.

For brands, this is just unacceptable. However, there is a way to get your profile photo to be your logo and to insert it digitally, so that it is as high-quality as possible. We will get into that in Chapter Four.

CHAPTER THREE:

USING SNAPCHAT – THE BASICS

Now that you've signed up for a Snapchat and your brand is on the app, you are going to need to know how to use the application. In this chapter, we're only going to go over the basics – the things you need to know to get around and check out the some of the buttons and knobs. In subsequent chapters, we will cover more advanced features and some things in further detail, including some of the features the businesses are going to be using the most.

NAVIGATION

The first thing that you need to know is how to navigate Snapchat successfully. So go to your app and open it and follow along as we discuss how you navigate through the Snapchat interface. When you enter the application, the first thing you'll see is your camera, either facing you are facing away from you, depending on what you've set it at. It is very easy to change the camera view. If you wanted to take a selfie instead a picture of what is in front of you, all you do is touch the little smiley face surrounded by arrows in the top right of your camera screen. Is very easy to hit this accidentally, which is why you may see your camera facing front are facing you when you login.

Navigating is done with swipes. If you swipe right you will see your contacts list, which is probably just team Snapchat right now. You can tap on the little speech bubble at the top right corner of the screen to chat with your contacts and you can search them by touching the magnifying glass. This is particularly useful if you have lots and lots of people in your contact list and you need to find a specific person.

If you swipe left you will see the stories that have been posted. The major brands – or the ones that have become a Snapchat partner on the top row while the other stories are from live events under the word 'live.'

If you swipe down from your home screen you will see your Snapchat QR code which is the yellow icon with the ghost in the middle. Those dots that you see there send a message to mobile devices of users that want to follow you and make it very easy to follow someone. This is one of the revolutionary new methods of adding followers the Snapchat is come up with. As you can see there are several features on here. You see your trophies for example, see who added you and add other people and then get a list of your friends.

You also notice that there is a gear icon in the top right corner. Tapping this will allow you to view your personal information and if you scroll down you'll see the login verification setting. This is where you will enter the code that they sent you via your mobile device. If you chose not to add a phone number they have you solve a puzzle instead to prove that you're human being.

That is all are going to cover for now. We will get into the more advanced features in the next couple chapters. If you are a brand and you want a quick start help guide to get you on Snapchat as quickly as possible, the next chapter covers the features that businesses need to know.

CHAPTER FOUR:

USING SNAPCHAT – FEATURES BUSINESSES USE THE MOST

As mentioned in the last chapter, we are now going to go over a couple of the features that businesses use the most, namely the logo and QR code. This is intended as sort of a quick start process. The basics in the last chapter were intended to get you navigating around the application successfully and this chapter will demonstrate how to use your QR code and a workaround for the lack of ability to upload your brand's logo to your profile directly.

YOUR LOGO AND QR CODE

Adding your logo to your Snapchat is going to take some creativity. That's because Snapchat doesn't allow you to upload a logo. What it does allow you to do is take up picture – which is actually a series of five pictures taken one right after the other – of your face or whatever you want. So, you can take a picture of your logo and it will be on your Snapchat profile and QR code. You should either find a way to take a picture with the camera that is perfectly still – and very high quality – or come up with some creative way to take a picture of your logo with the five snapshots which will be strung together to make a short GIF.

As for your QR code, it is intended to be something that you share in the real world and allow people to take pictures of to add you on

Snapchat. You can add your logo to your QR code image that you have to be careful doing it so that you don't mess up the code embedded within the dots that allows Snapchat to recognize your brand from that QR code.

The first thing that you're going to do is <u>download your QR code</u>, which requires you to go to that link (which is the Snapchat website), login to your Snapchat account and then download your QR code. Then, you can either take it into Photoshop yourself (and Photoshop is recommended for this particular project because of the layers function) and magically erase the white ghost and then put your logo on the layer below it so that it can be seen through the transparency of the ghost. You could also find someone on Fiverr to do it for you if you don't have Photoshop or don't want to use it. There are some pretty specific guidelines that you need to follow however, and if you're outsourcing this project, make sure that you share these with the person.

- ➢ Do not alter the shape of the ghost and do not break the black border. (Or remove it) around the ghost. This will cause your QR code to fail and people will not be able to use it to follow you on Snapchat.
- ➢ Don't stretch the box and anyway for change the shape of it.
- ➢ Don't invert the colors to try to be different.

➢ Do not print on glossy paper or cardstock because the shine may prevent people from those days, scanning your code.

Then, you just put up the QR code anywhere you want – your website, social media platforms and everywhere online, but also in the real world. You can have the QR code blown up and posted on the wall at your brick-and-mortar store(s), you can even put it on your business cards. You might even be able to put it on a billboard or on the side of company vehicles, but you should test that thoroughly before spending any significant amount of money on it.

There are other features that businesses use, such as the story feature, but we're going to get into that subject in Chapters Six and Eight.

CHAPTER FIVE:

USING SNAPCHAT – ADVANCED FEATURES

In this chapter, we're going to go over some of the more advanced features of Snapchat. We're going to skip things that will be covered in later chapters like stories but this chapter will allow you to use the basic functions of Snapchat like the videos and pictures to get you started in the platform's world.

USING ZOOM IN YOUR VIDEOS

You don't have to take a standard picture or video with Snapchat. By default, the videos is zoomed all the way out but all you have to do to zoom in is use two fingers and pull them apart just like if you are zooming in on a webpage on your phone. Zooming out is the opposite; bring your fingers together. One other small side note: if you haven't found it yet, the control to flip your camera from front-facing to rear-facing is on the top right of your video screen.

USING YOUR OWN PHOTOS

In case you didn't know, you can use the photos that are in your phone's library to use in one-to-one communication in a direct message. All you do is swipe right on any friend that you want to send a picture to and tap on the blue bubble at the left side of the screen when it comes in the frame. Your private chat will open with them and you can tap on the yellow circle like you're getting ready to take a picture, and when your camera comes up, look at the bottom right where you will see the last photo that you took and you can tap on it and open your library. Then insert whatever photo from your library you want and share it as a snap.

IMPROVING YOUR SNAPS AND VIDEOS

You probably already know that you can add a caption to your picture video. After all, the app sometimes asks you if you want to leave a caption when you click the shutter button; (if it doesn't, you can click the 'T' at the top). But did you know there are actually ways that you can improve your caption? Here are the ways that you can make your snaps and videos look amazing.

You can change the size of your caption text as well as the placement. All you have to do is after you type your caption, type the 'T' a second time and it will make your text much larger and thicker. If you tap it again, it will center your text. If you want to make your text even bigger then use the same spreading your fingers motion that you used to zoom and make it as big as you like. Make sure that you put each finger on the end of the text; it may take a few practice tries. You can then experiment with moving the text around and resizing it to create anything you want.

You probably saw the icon that looks like a piece of paper to the left of the text icon, and the one on the right that looks like a pencil or pen. The one on the left is the comprehensive list of emojis that Snapchat has to offer. You can choose an emoji, and then resize it just like you did with the text as well as move it around, rotate it or anything you like. If you tap on the pencil icon at allows you to choose a color and then write with your finger (or a stylus if you have one) on your snap. You can find a list of the emojis and what they mean online.

Another thing that you can do is go to your settings menu and turn on geofilters. All you do is go down to additional services and tap manage and it will allow you to enable filters. Once you have done this you can go back to your picture and it will ask you – or rather tell you – that you can swipe right for filters. Filters differ with each geographical zone which is why Snapchat asked for your ZIP Code when you enable them. Go through the filters that are available and see if there any you like.

There are a couple of neat things that you can do that we will end the chapter with. First, if you tap on the words in your caption you will notice that tapping on one word will underline it then you can tap the word and hold and it will highlight it. Then you can change the color of that individual word to whatever you want. This is particularly useful if you want to use letters as frames. You can play with this and find what works best for you but an example is making the 'O' large enough to where most of it is out of frame and the part that is left frames your picture in an oval. Finally, another advanced feature that you should know about is that once per day you can replay someone's snap. However, it has to be the last snap that you viewed. You will see the option to replay on your screen after the snap expires.

CHAPTER SIX:

INTRODUCTION TO MARKETING ON SNAPCHAT

Marketing on Snapchat is a little unusual and it is centered around the story feature. We will get into the actual construction of stories in Chapter 8; the purpose of this chapter is to show you how you market with stories.

The first thing you should know is what a story actually is. That requires understanding a little bit of Snapchat terminology if you haven't already learned it. A snap is a video or picture that you send a specific person. Although you certainly can advertise with snaps, they are only going to one person at a time and they disappear in no more than 10 seconds. This makes it an almost unusable marketing tool – even if it were lucrative to send snaps to your existing friends list. Of course, it's not lucrative and that's the point. So, we won't worry about snaps in this chapter.

However, we *are* going to discuss stories. The difference between a story and a snap is that stories contain multiple images and video and stay available for viewing for 24 hours. The other difference is that while you can send snaps to just people on your friends list (or the rare person that is enabled everyone to send them snaps) you stories can be viewed by anyone you choose. You can set your account to allow anyone to view your stories. Since stories can be shared, they are a great marketing strategy.

SETTING YOUR ACCOUNT SO EVERYONE CAN VIEW YOUR STORIES

This is something, as you may have guessed, that can be done in your settings menu. So swipe down and when you get to the page where it allows you to see who has added you, click on the settings gear at the top right. Then go down to where you can change both who can send you snaps and who can view your stories.

So now you are ready to start sharing stories on Snapchat. You may not know how to build a story yet, but that's okay because are going to cover that in Chapter 8. Make sure that you let other social media networks know when you post a story because you will have Snapchat users on those networks and they will log in and check out your story. If your story is geared towards some sort of product or service you definitely want as many people viewing it as possible, so don't rely on just Snapchat to get views. However, keep in mind to always be entertaining so that users will want to share your story with others, and will come back for the next one.

CHAPTER SEVEN:

GETTING YOUR INITIAL FOLLOWING

If you want to be successful in marketing on Snapchat then you're going to need to get a following. Just like with your Twitter and Facebook followers, the more people that you have following you, the higher the chances that other people will follow you. This chapter will give you some tips on getting your first followers on Snapchat as well as some things not to do to get followers.

LET YOUR CREATIVITY FREE

The first thing that you want to do is make sure that anything that you're posting is creative and fun and shows off your artistic expressions. Posting boring content with text that is always the same never changes, over the same boring videos of products are going to get exactly nowhere with Snapchat. But pictures of people using your product in unconventional ways, with your caption and emojis, is going to get people's interest and make them want to share your content.

USE YOUR OTHER SOCIAL NETWORKS

We discussed this a little bit in the last chapter but it might be useful to understand exactly how you should use your social networks to get Snapchat followers. The best way to do it is to come up with compelling things to post on your Twitter, Facebook, Instagram or whatever social network you're using. These are teaser items such as a promo code within the story that you can only get if you go to Snapchat.

PUT YOUR SNAPCODE EVERYWHERE

Place your snapcode or Snapchat information anywhere that you can. Post it on your website, around your store if you have one and anywhere else that you can think of where people that you want to influence would be willing to join Snapchat or are already using it. You also put it on your business cards, put a link to it in your email or even advertise on forums that are in your industry.

USE SOCIAL MEDIA INFLUENCERS

Do you know a YouTuber or someone who has a large following online but isn't necessarily Hollywood celebrity? Do you think they are someone that would be interested in your product or service? You might be able to leverage influencers by offering them something special which they will almost always talk about afterward and you can get followers from that.

THINGS NOT TO DO TO GET FOLLOWERS ON SNAPCHAT

There are a few things that you shouldn't do to get followers on Snapchat. One of them is to use one of the services offered on websites like Fiverr that promise to get you thousands of followers. For one thing, they are not going to buy anything from you and may not even have real people behind them. Also, you might get your Snapchat account banned by doing so at some point in the future. You also should try not to be boring and make sure that you're accessible in some way because users don't want a shadowy face in the background, they want a real live human being behind your company that they can interact with.

CHAPTER EIGHT:

BUILDING FANS THROUGH STORIES

You're going to use stories to do more than advertise your products or services. Think of a story like a viral video. You know if you make it overly promotional it's not going to work. You want something clever, something that no one has ever seen and something that evokes emotion in a human being. This will make them want to share with their friends and it will give you the exposure that you're looking for. But creating good stories will also make people want to follow you so every time you create a story keep in mind that you are both trying to get people to follow you and you're trying to get your product or service out there.

CREATING AMAZING STORIES

If you want to know how to create a great Snapchat story then go online and look at some of the best ones that have ever been made. There are lots of Snapchat stories that have been featured on websites like Buzzfeed, Mashable or even some of the more conventional media out there. As you look through those Snapchat stories and laugh, try to think of ways in which you can incorporate a similar campaign on your own Snapchat account that would both be entertaining and promote your product or service a little.

Stories can not only be told in photos, they can also include video. You can come up with a clever idea to pair the video with the snapshots if you like. There are lots of ways to create a good story but it starts with a good idea. Sit down with employees or even your friends and try to come up with a Snapchat story that would be funny. Use anything for inspiration; go to Google search and type in a random word and look at the images that come up with that word. Look around your environment and see if there's anything there that amuses you. Think about the last thing that you found funny and why you liked it. There are lots of ways to come up with great ideas for stories.

Sit down and storyboard out your story, which means that you decide which order your snaps and videos are going to go in, before you even take them in some cases, and then make sure that you have the right order and a compelling story that is going to keep people clicking the next button. Remember, just like with YouTube videos, you shouldn't go over a few minutes in length. Otherwise, people are going to get bored. Now, you can get to work making great stories on Snapchat!

CHAPTER NINE:

DISCOVER – SNAPCHAT'S PARTNER PROGRAM

One thing you may be interested in knowing about is Snapchat's partner program called Discover. This program is pretty much out of reach for anyone who isn't a major brand because of the $750,000 (per day) price tag, but there are actually other ways to get on Discover then by being a partner with Snapchat.

Some of the major brands are letting other brands advertise on their Discover space for a lot less than they are paying for their Discover spot. This is a way for the brands that are advertising on Discover to get some of the money back that they are spending and it is a great way for anyone with about $50,000 to spend to get a huge amount of exposure.

For smaller brands, unfortunately there is nothing yet that they can do to start advertising with Snapchat. There would have to be some sort of major overhaul to the application if they were going to start allowing people to advertise on snaps and videos and other places around the site. Right now, there is nothing that is the equivalent of Facebook advertising for small businesses and people with products or services to promote but that may be coming in the future. Snapchat has only recently been able to get enough followers to command the kind of rates that they are getting from their Discover program.

So the bottom line here is, if you have a great deal of money to spend on advertising then Snapchat may be exactly what you need – or at least advertising on one of the brands that are currently on or will be on Snapchat's Discover program in the near future. If you have a small business or you just want to advertise products and services, then you should use Snapchat for marketing purposes in the ways that we discussed in this book rather than advertising on the platform.

CHAPTER TEN:

VIEWING STATISTICS

Another thing that you're going to want to do what it comes to Snapchat is find out what kind of statistics you can get and how you can use them to make your brand better. Unfortunately Snapchat doesn't really offer any sort of detailed analytics or anything to tell you who is visiting your story page, but it does have some statistics that you might find useful. In this article were going to go over those as well as tell you about the alternatives that are cropping up that may give you the analytics information that you need.

There are several metrics that Snapchat offers you. The first one that we're going to discuss here is the total unique views that a story has gotten – and stories are the only analytics that we will discuss here because that's what you will be using as a marketer and also it is the only feature on the site that Snapchat offers analytics on.

Total unique views tell you how many people opened up your story and saw at least the first frame. They may not of gone on to finish the story and in fact may not have even when past that first frame but it tells you how many people opened up your story and it is very accurate. The thing about stories is that you can see how many views are on every single frame of the story – or on the video if you created a video

– and that's how you get these total unique views – you go to the first frame and look.

The second analytic that were going to discuss is total story completions. You get your total story completions by going to the very last frame of your story and taking a look how many people finished your story. Make sure that you're keeping track of these metrics as you see them and also keep in mind is this will be after the 24 hours that your story has been live.

The third analytic is probably the most important of all of these and it's the completion rate which you'll figure out yourself by looking at your total unique views compared to your total story completions. So for example, if you had 1000 people start your story but only 450 completed it you would have a 45% completion rate; the higher that your rate is, the better your story.

Finally, the fourth analytic that were going to discuss is the stopping point. You want to look at your snaps and try to figure out if there is a trend as to when they stopped watching or viewing your story. If you can detect a trend at a certain frame then you will have discovered where the problem was – which means the problem was somewhere up to that point not necessarily the frame that they stopped on.

Companies That Are Providing Analytics Information

There are a few companies out there that are providing analytics information for Snapchat. They have only popped up recently, but they have some innovative programs and several have very good reputations with businesses that are looking to market on Snapchat. If you want to find out what is going on with your Snapchat account and have detailed analytics so that you can make the best decisions possible on what to post and when as well as what's working and what isn't, then you might want to look into using one of these companies. Just do your research and make sure that other people are recommending the service and that the price isn't outrageous compared to the going rate.

CHAPTER ELEVEN

USING SNAPCHAT AT LIVE EVENTS TO GET FOLLOWERS

In this chapter, were going to discuss a couple of ways that you can use live events to get followers to your Snapchat account. The first thing that you should do is open up your Snapchat app and look where the Discover page is. You will see a place where it says live and then you will find stories below that. Don't get confused by this live event feature that Snapchat has.

They do a thing called Our Story where they pick a live event that's going on and then take people's snaps and video from that event and build a curated story that everyone can see regardless of who they are following. That is not the type of live event that will be discussing in this chapter. The type of live event that you want to use Snapchat for is the kind of live event where your company is doing something exciting that customers can attend. You can hold these events whenever you like, and you can use Snapchat to both bring people to your live event and convince people that are already at your live event to sign up and follow you on Snapchat.

The way that you get people from your Snapchat to your live event is fairly straightforward. Just build a story using snaps in that event and invite people out. Just remember, stories last for 24 hours so the best way for you to do a live event with Snapchat stories is have the story begin before the live event starts – 24 hours before the start of your event. Then you can start a brand-new story when the event starts and people will be able to check out live images and video from the event.

Obviously, this is a great way to get people to your event because you not only get people that have to prepare for the event and are willing to come 24 hours after hearing about it, but you also get people who are more of right-here-right-now, fly by the seat of your pants people. In other words, people who will come to your live event on very short notice.

It is worth noting that this will only work if you have followers in the same city that you are doing the event in and if you are a large brand and you are in a large city this is usually not a problem. For small businesses, many of their followers will have followed them by coming into their brick-and-mortar store and so they will not have a problem either. In fact, the only people who are going to have a problem are the people who do not have a brick-and-mortar store and only work online but have a very small business and not a huge Snapchat following. Holding a live event will be very poorly attended because very few of your Snapchat followers are likely to be in that particular area.

In either case, whether you are convincing people to sign up and follow you on Snapchat from your live event, or you are trying to convince followers in that area to come to your live event, you should definitely use some sort of promotion, coupon or giveaway to entice them.

CHAPTER TWELVE

USING SNAPCHAT TO DELIVER PERSONAL CONTENT

This chapter is designed to give you some ideas on how you can deliver personal content to the people who follow you on Snapchat, including what kind of content you can deliver and some ideas for some great personal deliveries, as well as tips on how you should deliver them.

This is something that you would do individually with your followers and is designed to work with a promotion that you have going on. For example, suppose that you posted on your website that sometime in the next few days you are going to give away a certain number of free items or gift certificates but that the people who would receive them would be followers on Snapchat whom you sent a personal snap to.

What you should do next, is choose a specific day during that week and even choose the hours that you will be doing it between. Then you can ramp up your advertising efforts a little during that period because you know that the people that are following you on Snapchat are paying attention because they want to get a free item and they will read your stories more frequently. This is just one way that delivering personal content can help your business.

Another way that you can use personal contact to grow your business is by thanking customers when they purchase something from your website by sending them a snap and then create a story with those snaps. This is a great method because all it requires is that you asked people on your order form to put in their Snapchat ID.

There are many different ways out there of using personal communication to grow your business. You can try to get referrals from the people who are currently following you by creating a story that tells them that they will get something at a huge discount or for free if they can get a certain number of people to follow you on Snapchat. You may have to have them post on another social media network – Twitter is the best option – because you may not see it on Snapchat if they snap and send you the name of a user that followed you based on their recommendation. You can ask them to post the person's Snapchat ID on Twitter with a specific hashtag and then you can check your Snapchat followers to find out if that person has joined that day and then you can then give them credit for the follow.

Honesty Power! Local Directories Work All You Need to Know **By Oscar Smith**

Chapter Thirteen: Give Followers an Inside Look

Another great way that you can use Snapchat is to provide your followers with some behind-the-scenes information or an inside look at something that you're doing. This has a number of benefits, first and foremost being that the people who follow you on Snapchat will pay closer attention to your snaps and stories and will keep your business in mind if they need your product or service because you are already in their mind. But another benefit is that if you're behind the scenes information is exciting, and whatever you're building or doing is compelling, people are going to want to share it.

There are lots of ways that you can use this. First of all, make sure that all of the other social media you use knows that you're posting exclusive scenes information on Snapchat. That means that if the followers from your other social media platforms want to see the behind-the-scenes information, they are going to become followers on Snapchat as well, which gives you more followers. You can use this several ways to get followers every time you have something that you can show behind the scenes information of.

You can even drive traffic to your own website using Snapchat. If you snap and build stories you can place a method for getting to your website within the story as well as a reason for them to go there – a call to action that is going to give them some sort of benefit. You always want to make sure that you have some sort of benefit to offer them. One great way to use Snapchat to get some long-term results is to direct them to your website and have them sign up for your mailing list. That means that you can now send emails and people will look at an email much longer than they will a tweet or a snap story most of the time.

The main thing here is that you just make sure that you are always interacting with your audience. If you have something that you think that would be great on Snapchat, make sure you put it on there. Make sure that you take every opportunity that you have to give people that follow you on social media some sort of inside information about your company or something that they didn't have before. If you want them to do something and follow a call to action, then make sure that you are offering some sort of benefit to do so as well.

CHAPTER FOURTEEN

RUNNING CONTESTS & PROMOTIONS ON SNAPCHAT

Snapchat is a great place to run contests and promotions. Many of the other businesses that are on Snapchat use this method to both say thanks – usually with discounts – and to get more followers by stirring up some excitement. So, how do you run a contest or promotion that will do well on Snapchat? In this chapter, we'll explore some of the ways that you can use this type of marketing on Snapchat and some of the benefits that you can get from it.

DESIGNING YOUR PROMOTION

The first thing you're going to have to do is design your promotion. You need to figure out what kind of things are going to require from the customers or followers and how you are going to set it up logistically. For example, they could add you as a friend on Snapchat and then you could request them to create a video or take a snapshot and send it to you.

PROMOTING YOUR PROMOTION

Now you're going to promote your contest. You can promote it in your brick-and-mortar store, on your own website and on the other social media platforms that you use. There are all kinds of ways that you can promote your contest but you do want to keep in mind that you have to let your followers know in a very clear fashion if you decide to use their videos later on in a future promotion.

CHECKING YOUR CONTEST ENTRIES

The next step in the process is checking your contest entries. For example, if you had your users send you videos one of the things that you can do to make sure that you see all of the entries is to use a third-party program to view the videos and save them to your phone. You are probably aware by now that if you use Snapchat and someone sends you a video or a snap, it is going to self-destruct in no more than 10 seconds unless they build a story with it in which case it will be gone in 24 hours.

From there is just a matter of figuring out who the winner is in your promotion or however you designed it – with multiple winners or with everyone receiving some sort of promotional code – however you choose to create a fun and exciting promotion that your followers will like. If you can do this, you will find that the followers that you have will be much more apt to check out your snaps and videos as well as stories when you post them.

CHAPTER FIFTEEN

ALIGNING YOURSELF WITH NICHE INFLUENCERS ON SNAPCHAT

One of the ways that you may not have considered marketing your company with Snapchat is to use niche influencers. This is actually a tried-and-true method of marketing and it is something that big companies do quite often. Some companies have partnered with YouTube stars in the past who work in the same niche as them – such is cosmetic companies pairing up with extremely popular makeup tutorial YouTubers – and so it is a very good way to market your company.

WHAT ARE NICHE INFLUENCERS?

So, what are niche influencers? They are people who have a lot of influence over a large number of potential customers within your own niche. Niche influencers often have large followings that go out and buy their recommended products and trust them implicitly. When it comes to anything that they use personally, followers will go out and buy that particular product in droves, which is why brands send popular YouTubers free samples of their products all the time.

BENEFITS OF USING NICHE INFLUENCERS

There are a lot of benefits to using niche influencers. For one thing, you are going to have a chance to entice their audience to come over to your particular company when they need a product or service that you provide. For another, the name of your company will be going around within circles that make up your industry.

HOW TO USE NICHE INFLUENCERS

So, how should use niche influencers? There are many creative ways that you can do this. Some people send them free samples of whatever products or services that they are selling – as long as that particular influencer is in your industry that is perfectly acceptable – and others do things like allowing a well-known person to take over a social media account. In fact that is something that is been quite a trend recently.

HOW TO FIND NICHE INFLUENCERS

Finding niche influencers within your particular industry isn't all that difficult. You can use websites like Klout, Peer Index and Cred or any of the other barometers of influence that are out there. You can also check social media and find out who has a huge following within your particular industry. There are various ways to go about this depending on what social media platforms that you use but you definitely should check Twitter, Insta Graham, Pinterest and Facebook. Of course, you may be able to find out who the niche influencers are within your industry that are also on Snapchat.

CHAPTER SIXTEEN

MEASURING YOUR SUCCESS WITH SNAPCHAT

So how do you measure your success with Snapchat? Knowing whether or not a campaign was successful, will depend on coming up with creative ways that you can figure out whether or not something worked. For example, if you did a Snapchat marketing campaign and you asked the users on that platform to do something on a different platform, then it would be very easy to measure your success – or at least the numbers. However, there is more to success than the numbers and we'll get into that here.

FIRST, LET'S TALK ABOUT THE NUMBERS

Obviously, the numbers are important. But there is a great deal more to be aware of. Before you can get into any of that however, you need to know the numbers and so you are going to have to come up with some method of figuring out how many people you reached on Snapchat and how many of them took your call to action and actually follow through with signing up for an email list, posting a tweet with a certain hashtag or whatever particular method that you are using. You can make use of the Snapchat tools that were discussed in the chapter on analytics as well as your own methods of counting people that have responded.

NOW, LET'S TALK ABOUT THE DEMOGRAPHICS

So, you are going to have to figure out some way that you can get demographic information from the people that are responding to your marketing campaigns. Demographics are super important when it comes to campaigns because if you know what type of people have responded to a particular product or service, or advertising campaign, then you know how to improve it next time. Demographics can be difficult to get in the best way is probably to go with one of the companies that were discussed in the chapter on analytics because there is really no way to get that information with your own efforts.

NOW, LET'S TALK ABOUT USER RESPONSE

The last thing that you want to measure is how the users felt about the particular marketing campaign that you did. You want to know what they thought of the campaign itself and also, you should try to find out whether they were happy to sign up for your mailing list because the offer was terrific or whether they were on the fence about it. Finding out how users responded to a particular marketing campaign can go a long way in helping you improve future marketing campaigns and get better responses.

CHAPTER SEVENTEEN

LEARNING FROM OTHER BRANDS ON SNAPCHAT

You should definitely learn from other brands on Snapchat. There are several ways to do this but with the platform constantly evolving and with new marketing ideas coming all the time it can be a little time-consuming to keep up with everything. However you do want to make an effort to try to figure out what other companies are doing – particularly the biggest companies because those are going to be the easiest ones to find and will save you a little time. Figure out what other brands did and then come up with methods that work just as well. In this chapter, were going to come up with some ways that you can find out what other brands are up to and learn from them.

NEWS ARTICLES

If you follow marketing news, you are definitely going to find people talking about Snapchat. With 2 million active users per month there are a lot of people with their eye on this particular application who want to see where it is going – particularly since the company refused Facebook's offer. So if you look at the marketing news websites where you set up your new search for Snapchat you should build a find some great information on what some of the major brands are up to when it comes to Snapchat.

ASK OTHER PEOPLE IN THE INDUSTRY

Another thing that you can do is ask other people that you know are in the industry. Regular communication with professionals like yourself that are within the same industry that you are in will allow you to share a great deal of information with each other that you might not have had on your own. People that are within your own industry are easy to find and unless they are direct competitor there probably going to be very happy to discuss their methods.

FOLLOW MARKETING BLOGS THAT ARE ALL ABOUT THE TRENDS

Find some great marketing blogs that have good information and then sign up to get regular updates or an RSS feed from them. Bloggers will do quite a bit of research regularly and so they may be able to get information before you can on some of the trends that are going on in Snapchat. You can use Google search to find bloggers who concentrate particularly on Snapchat and on the marketing that goes with it.

CHAPTER EIGHTEEN

INTEGRATING SNAPCHAT WITH YOUR SITE & SOCIAL MEDIA

Depending upon what type of site you have, adding Snapchat to it could be very easy or could be quite difficult. There are so many platforms out there now for creating a website and content management systems like WordPress are not the only players in the DIY world of website creation. In this chapter, were going to discuss how you can integrate Snapchat with your website and with your social media.

If you have a WordPress website being able to integrate Snapchat will depend upon the theme that you have. While all of the current themes definitely have places for Facebook, Twitter, Pinterest and others that are more well-known, not very many of the themes out there have automatic places where you can put your Snapchat information. However, you can put your Snapchat ID and even your QR code on the sidebar of your WordPress site by using a text widget.

If your website is built from scratch with HTML then you may have to get your web designer to create a place for your Snapchat QR code and for the user information that you want to post on your website. You should definitely put the QR code in the header of your homepage so that people can easily take a picture of it and try to follow you on Snapchat whenever they visit your website.

Integrating your Snapchat into your social media is going to take some creativity on your part. There really isn't any place that you can post your QR code and Snapchat information on Twitter. The only thing that you could do is replace your profile picture with your QR code but this is probably a bad idea for several reasons – one Twitter might not be happy that you're using a competing social media site's QR code on their site and Snapchat might not be happy about it either.

There is also the fact that you should have a decent profile picture on your Twitter account. One idea that may work on both Twitter and Facebook is putting your QR code within the background – in twitter that means the background that your tweets are sitting on and on Facebook you would have to put it in the larger header profile.

Just make sure that you aren't being obtrusive so that the social media website doesn't have to you about putting a QR code from a different social network onto their site – which they usually don't – and don't forget to remind people within your social media feeds as well as integrating it into the platform.

YOUTUBE
ADS EXCELLENCE

PART THREE

YOUTUBE ADVERTISING

CHAPTER 1:
AN INTRODUCTION TO YOUTUBE ADVERTISING

YouTube is one of the most under-utilized platforms by many digital marketers. Despite many statistics *clearly* showing the profitability of video marketing, even many of the web's pre-eminent digital marketers are shy to get involved.

Why is this? Simple: many marketers who are working from home lack the resources, the know-how or the confidence to get involved with video marketing.

But you know what? That's *exactly* why you need to get involved and why you need to learn to use this critical tool.

Leaving the statistics to one side for a moment, video marketing is incredibly valuable simply because it allows you to change the way that others perceive your business. When you create a great video with high production values, you make your organization appear far more professional, stable and resourceful. Instead of looking like you're 'some guy' writing articles from his Mum's basement, you'll now look like a real business complete with high production values and a professional sheen that inspires trust and confidence in your brand.

At the same time, video marketing also has some other advantages. For example: it's highly engaging beyond what you can achieve with a written advert or even a blog post. Think about how often you have sat up all night watching TV programs that you weren't really interested in *simply* because it was too difficult to turn off and turn your attention away from them.

Videos combine sound, music, image and clever editing and they let us speak *directly* to the audience. If you're a digital marketer with a personal brand and you're trying to gain the trust and familiarity with your audience, then going on video and letting them 'meet' you that way is incredibly valuable. Likewise, though, if you're a large a corporation and you want to show off your products, then being able to put them on the screen and show them being used will make it much easier for your audience to understand them and to see the appeal and the value proposition.

Think about what you'd be more likely to buy: something you heard described in a piece of text, or something you could see being held up to the camera, being used and shot in dynamic, flattering lighting. Add in some great music to underscore the value of the item and a great, persuasive sales script and you can make anything seem incredibly desirable.

YOUTUBE ADVERTISING

And one of the most effective forms of video marketing available to any internet marketer is YouTube advertising. YouTube is a *massive* platform and provides incredible reach to a vast range of different users across the world. The only downside is that it is also very difficult to get noticed through YouTube. As with running a blog, creating a YouTube channel means competing with millions of other content creators and saturation in almost every niche imaginable.

This is where YouTube advertising comes in. Using a YouTube advertising campaign, you can ensure that millions of people see your video *instantly*. This can then be used to directly sell a product, to drive traffic to your website, or even to drive traffic to a YouTube channel.

In other words, YouTube advertising allows you to quickly 'skip' the hard work normally associated with building your channel and instead get straight to the part where you begin getting huge exposure and building your brand.

SOME STATISTICS

In case you're not yet convinced that YouTube is the platform for you, it may help to look at some of the incredible statistics surrounding the video sharing site.

For instance, did you know that YouTube has over *one billion* users. That makes it absolutely massive and to put it in perspective, is nearly a third of everyone on the internet.

Every single day, these users together watch hundreds of millions of hours of video on the channel and on mobile alone, YouTube manages to reach more 18-34 year olds and 18-49 year olds than any cable network in the US.

So in other words, if you were thinking of spending money on a video advertising campaign, then your money would actually be *much* better spent on YouTube advertising. This is especially true too considering that YouTube advertising is far more affordable.

Think these numbers are impressive now? Then you'll be even more impressed to learn that the user base is still growing exponentially. In fact, it grows by more than *three times* year on year. That means that there will likely be three times as many users by the end of next year. Between March 2014 and January 2016, the number of users on YouTube increased by a whopping 40%.

These users are also spread throughout the world, which is great if you have an international product. 80% of YouTube's viewers come from outside the US in fact and the channel is available in over 76 different languages.

More than half of YouTube's views are from mobile devices but it's also worth taking into consideration just how popular YouTube is across a range of other devices as well. YouTube can be enjoyed on TVs and even on games consoles, so it's available even in households without computers or smartphones.

People don't just use YouTube for entertainment either – they likewise use it for looking up information and getting answers to questions. YouTube is commonly used just like Google as a search engine and is in fact the *second largest* search engine after Google in terms of the number of searches.

For all these reasons, YouTube actually controls the flow of 17% of all internet traffic.

ADVERTISING

And advertisers and creators are profiting greatly from all this success. Partner revenue has been increasing by 50% year on year and channels earning six figures a year from YouTube have also increased by the same amount.

Adoption of YouTube advertising is growing too. The number of advertisers using YouTube has increased by 40% each year and the average spend for the top 100 advertisers has increased by 60%.

What does this tell us? Well for now, it tells us that YouTube advertising still isn't oversaturated. There's still space here and especially for internet marketers. If you use YouTube marketing to show videos of your new eBook or your self-development blog, then you will be one of the few marketers using it that way currently. This in turn means you can stand out and get attention and you can get great prices and excellent ROI for your campaign.

Similarly though, it also shows you that companies already using YouTube advertising are profiting from it and are thus reinvesting *more* money into it. Did you know that every single one of the top 100 global brands have run YouTube adverts in the last year? TrueView adoption is growing too – and it grew by 45% over 2014.

This is the *perfect* time to set up an account and to start reaching bigger audience.

WHAT YOU WILL LEARN IN THIS BOOK

So without a doubt, YouTube advertising is one of the absolute *best* ways to engage with your audience, to drive traffic, to generate profit and to grow your brand.

But you may still be feeling apprehensive. Perhaps you're unsure as to whether you have what it takes to create videos of a professional quality, or maybe you don't know how to go about using the platform. Perhaps you're concerned about the amount of money you'd need to spend.

Don't be.

This is where this book will come in handy and will show you the ropes and *everything* you need to learn in order to start making the most from YouTube advertising. Throughout the course of this tome, you'll learn how to create stunning videos that have a professional quality without spending a huge amount of money. At the same time, you'll learn about key phrases and how to get maximum exposure with minimum spend. You'll learn the ins and outs of the different options available for creating YouTube ads and you'll learn how to integrate your advertising campaign with a great YouTube channel for maximum exposure.

CHAPTER 2

GETTING STARTED WITH YOUTUBE ADVERTISING

While the number of internet marketers currently using YouTube to its fullest is still quite slim, there are nevertheless some great examples of people who *are* making a lot of money from it. One example is the very 'visible' Mike Chang from Six Pack Shortcuts who uses a ton of advertising to drive visitors to his channel and to his information products. One of his most recent videos involved him stuffing his face as much as he could to demonstrate how his training methods don't require you to starve yourself.

The video is actually quite unpleasant to watch and is certainly fairly controversial. Both these things work in Mike's favour however, as both these things mean people are more likely to watch and to click through to see what the channel is all about. Remember: these videos will normally show just before fitness and bodybuilding videos that the user has clicked on and this is a great way for them to grab attention.

In some of his other YouTube ads, Mike will talk about free techniques that you can use as a reader to lose weight or build muscle. To see the free technique, you need to click on the ad to get directed to another video. This brings people to the Six Pack Shortcuts brand and is what is known as a 'sales funnel'. Gradually, viewers engage more and more with the brand until eventually they are willing to pay for the product.

Another example is Tai Lopez. If you spend much time on YouTube, then you'll no doubt have seen him talking about how he earned his Lamborghini in his garage. Once again, the video is fairly ostentatious and controversial and some people will be put off by it. Either way though, viewers end up watching and this technique has allowed Tai to very quickly grow his channel to 406,000 viewers plus.

It's actually doubtful though whether that Lamborghini is even his…

You don't need to be so on-the-nose, controversial or deceptive to make a splash though. Equally successful is the fitness channel 'Athlean-X' which promotes 'training like an athlete'. In the advertising campaign for this channel, owner Jeff Cavaliere actually actively challenges the methods of advertisers like Mike Chang and positions himself as the more grounded and scientific alternative.

The techniques you'll learn here will enable you to emulate the success these content creators have had and even to surpass them with your own products and channels.

SETTING UP YOUR ACCOUNT

Step 1: Creating Your YouTube Account

To get started with your advertising, you'll first need to create your account.

These days, YouTube is integrated very closely with Google and with Google+. That means that the easiest way to sign in, is just to log in with your standard Google account. From here, you will then have the option to create a specific YouTube account.

To create your channel, head over to 'All My Channels' and then find the dialogue box that says 'Create a New Channel'. So far, so self-explanatory!

Once you've created your channels coincidentally, you'll be able to find them all situated here. At the same time, you'll also be able to see your Google+ accounts underneath. If you want to create a new channel for your Google+ page, then you can do so by clicking on these.

This means that if you have a business on Google Plus, you can easily create a channel for that business and have your accounts linked. Either way, you need to be on Google Plus in order to use YouTube and in order to be able to add comments etc.

When you click to create your channel, you'll either use the name associated with your Google+ account, or you'll create a new name that's relevant to your brand and that's easy for your visitors to find and to understand. You may choose to create multiple channels – one for your brand and one for yourself as a personal user. Alternatively, you might choose to create multiple channels for each of your products. For instance, you may want to create one channel for your brand and another for your app – Microsoft for instance has a Microsoft account, as well as a Surface account and a Windows account etc.

Take a look over the terms and conditions and once you're happy with the name of the channel you can click 'done' to go ahead and publish the channel.

Step 2: Building Your Channel
Once you have created your channel, the next step is to create some content for it and to add some information.

In case you were wondering, your YouTube channel and your advertising campaign are going to be intimately linked so that when users click on your ads, they will very often be taken to your account page. This means you should make sure that your page is ready to receive said visitors before you start creating your ads.

When people visit your channel, they'll see a number of different headings and features that will tell them about your brand. One of the most important things here for instance is your description which will simply explain what your channel is all about and why people should stick around. This is also important for SEO or 'Search Engine Optimization'. In other words, the text that you include in this description will be at least partly responsible for helping you to achieve more visibility in searches both on Google and through YouTube itself. Make sure then to think about what the most relevant 'keywords' are for your topic and what you can include to encourage more people to find your channel.

Likewise, you can also link to your social media and your website and you can feature some other channels you like. All of this will help your brand to grow. By linking to your website for instance, you'll be able to drive traffic that way and thereby increase the number of people engaging with your brand.

Meanwhile, linking to your website and confirming it as yours will also allow you to link to products etc. directly from videos. As we will see later on, this is a rather useful feature for any marketer!

At the same time, linking to your social media will help you to drive more traffic still and will make it easier for you to build a cohesive brand across multiple platforms. One of the adages you most commonly hear with regards to internet marketing and social media marketing is to 'be everywhere'. Make sure you are in as many places as possible by creating a consistent brand on every platform you can find online.

This branding should extend as well to your cover image and your profile picture. The profile picture here is going to be the same as it is for your Google+ account, so make sure that this is something that accurately reflects your brand and your niche and that looks the part for your channel. The cover image meanwhile can be anything you choose, but a good bet is to put a logo of some sort front and to make sure this logo is the same across all of your channels (social media etc.).

As you create more content for your channel, you'll find that you're also able to add playlists of your videos, which will make it easier for visitors to find the type of information they're looking for. Another useful feature, is the ability to create a video that will promote your channel and this will play whenever anyone visits the page. Here you can create a montage of your best content or just talk to your visitors and explain what they can stand to learn by visiting your channel and why they should keep coming back.

Until you do this though, visitors will simply see a list of your recently added videos.

Depending on the strategy you intend to employ with your YouTube advertising, you will also need to create some content and start uploading videos. The ads you create are likely going to drive visitors to your channel and so you want to have some great content here waiting for them when they arrive.

We'll go into depth on how to create high quality videos on a shoestring budget later in this book. For now though, all you need to know is that your videos need to be high quality and they need to provide *value*. Don't worry about trying to sell or monetize just yet – what's most important is that you build a following and you gain the trust of your visitors. The best way to do *that* is to fill yourself with interesting and unique content that people will want to view and that will encourage them to subscribe. The more quality and value you provide, the more people will be interested in buying from you when you eventually come to sell something.

Step 3: Linking Your AdWords Account

Next you need to link your AdWords account to your YouTube account. This is the crucial step for YouTube advertising specifically and until you do this, your advertising and your YouTube will be separate entities from one another. Once you link the two, you'll not only be able to take part in YouTube advertising but you'll also have the option to see more statistics for your video such as 'earned videos'. You'll be able to control features like CTA overlays (more on this later) and remarketing.

In order to link these two accounts, you need to head over to your YouTube channel and then click the 'My Channel' tab after the channel icon. Now look for the 'Advanced' option and from here you should be able to find a tab that says 'Link an AdWords for Video Account'. This should have a 'Link an AdWords Account' link and when you click this, you'll be walked through the process of linking your AdWords account.

Of course, before you do this, you'll need to sign up to AdWords and create an account. You can also alternatively link your YouTube channel from within AdWords. TO do this, you need to sign into your AdWords account and then find the cog icon for settings. In here, you'll find an option that says 'Linked Accounts' and in there, you'll be able to find 'Link a YouTube Channel'. Click the channel you want to link and then search for the video you want to link to begin with.

CHAPTER 3:

CREATING YOUR FIRST VIDEO CAMPAIGN

Okay, now you've done all that, you're ready to start creating your first campaign and to start promoting a video of your choosing.

Read the following steps in order to learn how easy it is to start promoting your brand with YouTube advertising but don't do any of it just yet. We're going through this process as a learning curve for now and so that you understand how to get started. You'll want to read the rest of the book before you get to work though in order to ensure that your video ad is going to be as effective as possible and to ensure that you understand the precise workings of how the adverts work.

So with this all linked, you'll need to come up with a 'bidding strategy'. Most AdWords campaigns use a CPC or 'Cost Per Click' process which means that you only pay once the ad has been clicked. With YouTube though, you'll need to use something else called 'CPV'. That means 'cost per view' and in turn means that you only pay once the video is viewed all the way through.

We'll talk about this more in a moment but for now, all you need to know is that the amount you bid, is the amount you'll pay for each view. Your bid is your CPV, so it needs to be tied closely to your budget.

So why not just offer the very lowest CPV possible and that way get your ads at a very low price? Simple: because there are too many people trying to do the exact same thing and the amount you pay will directly impact on how visible your image is.

This is called 'bidding' because that's exactly how it works. You'll select the kind of content that you want your videos to appear on and once you do that, you'll be going up against all the other advertisers in your niche. YouTube will decide *which* advert to show based upon which of you is paying the most.

So this means that you can pay very little and get your adverts shown cheaply but not very often, or you can pay more and have your adverts seen much more frequently by a bigger audience. Of course the amount you're able to pay is likely to be dictated closely by the amount that you stand to earn from each video and how effective your campaign is at driving sales and profits.

Something else to recognize about the bidding process is that you won't always pay the maximum amount that you're willing to pay. As with bidding on eBay or at an auction, you're only required to *beat* the next highest bid. This means that you can set your CPV at $0.25 but if the next highest bid is $0.10, you'll only pay $0.11.

You'll also be able to set a budget that you won't go over. This is particularly useful if you have a limited budget as it guarantees that you won't spend more than you can afford. It also means you're capped out at a certain amount though – so if your daily spend is $10 and your CPV is $0.50, then there's a chance that you'll only get 20 views before your pool runs dry.

Unfortunately, there is no golden rule or ideal number to refer to when choosing your ad spend and ultimately the amount you bid will need to come down to your goals and objectives as well as your budget and cash flow.

You can of course set different bidding amounts for different campaigns though and this means that you can compare how two different campaigns are performing and try different strategies for each. What you also need to do is to generally track the performance of each of your campaigns and to look at how much they're earning and how much you're actually paying per click. You can then tweak the variables in order to make sure you have optimized your strategy.

This all means you need to think carefully about how to get the most out of your campaign and to get the most for your money. Another important factor to that end is your targeting.

Targeting refers to the way in which your ads will be aimed at a very specific group. Most advertising campaigns will have a particular target audience in mind and your job is to make sure that you're only paying for those specific people to see your ads.

TARGETING

If you are a video game developer and the digital product you are selling is an action platform game, then of course you're probably not going to want your adverts to show on videos aimed at hair and makeup. While there may be some overlap, these two interests are very different and generally appeal to different demographics. If you pay for your ad to appear in front of a makeup tutorial, then chances are you'll be wasting your money.

So instead, you want your video to appear only on relevant content and in this case that means you want it to turn up on videos like 'top 10 games' countdowns, on 'let's play' videos or on video game reviews. Someone watching a review of one video game is much more likely to click on your ad and buy *your* game.

On the other hand, if you are a selling an eBook on how to do your makeup perfectly, then you want your videos to appear before makeup tutorials and *not* before let's plays.

Targeting helps you to reach your specific target audience and in turn, this helps you to make more conversions and get a better ROI. But there is more to it than that as well; targeting also helps you to avoid facing so much competition and this in turn helps you to win more bids while spending less.

Put it this way: if your video is targeting a massive niche like bodybuilding, then you'll be going up against Mike Chang and Jeff Cavaliere, as well as countless other massive brands. This means you'll need to set a very high CPV and your budget will likely run out quickly.

But if your video ad is targeting something a lot more specific and niche – let's say 'food truck businesses' – then you can set your budget much lower and set your CPV much lower and still get seen by a lot of people. What's more, is that this smaller audience is much more likely to be interested in your product and thus convert into paying customers.

To set up topics, you simply choose from a couple of thousand different topics. This is somewhat limited when compared to regular AdWords that let you choose any keyphrases you want – however in some ways it also gives you more precise control and saves time.

Some of these categories are going to be very broad. These include the likes of 'Beauty and Fitness' or 'Face and Body Care'. These give you the most exposure but cost the most. But if you dig a little deeper into the sub categories then you can get more niche by choosing things like Face & Body Care, or Hygiene & Toiletries.

Another thing to think about when choosing your niche, is just which type of content is most abundant and most successful on YouTube.

Some video topics like makeup tutorials and 'let's play' videos come up time and time again, meaning there are more videos for you to appear on and those videos are likely to be higher profile. On the other hand, if you choose something that lends itself less well to videos – like programming – then you will be appearing on fewer videos.

CHOOSING YOUR AD

Once you've done all this, you'll then have the option to choose your advert and set it up. The first thing you need to consider here, is which *type* of advert you're going to use. There's actually multiple options in this regard and some will even allow you to earn money without creating an advert at all.

If you want to use traditional text ads, then you can have these appear on top of videos as they play. These look very similar to AdSense adverts (the ads that appear on websites) but are long and horizontal. These only show up on desktop mind, which means they won't be visible to the 50%+ of users who view on mobile (then again, desktop users may be more likely to convert for your specific type of content).

Overlay ads are a useful way to stand out from the pack and to reach a specific target audience without competing for the overcrowded space on Google's search engine results pages (SERPS). That said though, they also don't quite function in the same way as true video ads and don't have the same amount of engagement.

There are also ads called 'in-display ads' which show not *over* the video but next to it. These will appear right next to the feature video.

The more common type of ad though is the 'video ad' and that is what this book is mainly focussed on. There are many different types of video ad and these are charged differently – but we'll look at this in more detail later on.

For now, we'll focus on how you select your ad and set it up. To do this, you're basically going to upload the video to your YouTube channel (you can make it unlisted or private so that your subscribers don't get shown it) and then you're just going to select it as the video to go with that campaign.

This means you can actually use *any* video on your channel as your advert. If you want to, you can have a let's play as your ad! Of course this isn't going to drive many customers to your products though and it will likely be a waste of money. So *instead* you're better off creating a unique video that exists for the sole purpose of being an advert and generating revenue.

You'll also need to select the type of video ad, which in turn will dictate the behaviour of the video – you can learn more about this in the next chapter.

SETTING A DESTINATION

If someone clicks your advert, or if they click the branding that appears around it, then they're going to be taken to a specific destination which should encourage sales and engagement with your brand. It's up to you to choose what this destination is and it can either be your YouTube channel itself, or it can be another one of your videos. In other cases, you can link with a call to action, which means that you can send them straight to a landing page or site where they can then buy your product.

It's up to you how you want to set this up. If your aim is to increase engagement and to get more viewers and followers for long-term monetization, then linking them straight to your channel will give them the opportunity to see more of your content and to hopefully become fans/subscribers who will be more likely to buy from you in future. This is advantageous, as it can be somewhat difficult to convince people to buy products 'cold' if they've never heard of your brand before.

On the other hand though, if you are advertising a vacuum cleaner then you may be able to say everything you have to say in the video. In that case, sending someone straight to your online store where they can click 'buy' might be the best strategy!

Note that you also pay for a click – if someone doesn't watch your video all the way through but they click on the ad, then you're still going to pay for that at the price that you bid.

CHAPTER 4

HOW VIDEO ADS WORK

Video ads are of course adverts that are videos in themselves and this means they can be integrated much more seamlessly into the way YouTube operates. These are the main types of adverts on YouTube and the ones we're focussing on.

Again though, there are actually multiple different types of video ads for YouTube. YouTube calls this 'TrueView' and aims to give both the user and the advertiser more control over their campaigns as a result.

Choose this wisely, as the type of video ad that you choose is also going to impact on the options available for you in terms of your destinations and the cost.

IN-STREAM ADS

An in-stream advert for instance, is a video that will appear prior to the start of the target video. These pre-roll ads are like the adverts that play in a cinema before the main feature but there is one key difference that benefits both the advertisers *and* the users – which is that the videos are skippable.

As an advertiser, you can elect to make your video skippable after the first 5 seconds of the video. If the user clicks skip, then you don't pay for the view and the viewer isn't subjected to a message that doesn't relate to them. This makes your content *much* more targeted because people won't watch a long video all the way through if they're not at all interested in the subject matter and thus you'll avoid paying for those views!

If you're savvy though, you might now be thinking that perhaps there's a way for you to avoid ever paying – by making your video 100 minutes long so that no-one watched it through to the end. Nice try! But actually, so long as viewers stick around for 30 seconds, you will be paying for a view.

IN-SLATE ADS

An in-slate ad is only a little different to an in-stream ad. The key differentiating factor here is that the advert will be interspersed throughout the video that the users are watching. This means that your video will appear at pre-set points during another video that the video creator has chosen. This lets the creator set-up 'ad breaks' in their content and it also means that your video is going to appear on longer content rather than on short 30 second videos.

IN-SEARCH ADS

In-search ads meanwhile are adverts that appear in the search results above the 'organic results'. These ads normally have a yellow 'Ad' label next to them as well but they otherwise look like one of the videos on the channel with a little thumbnail.

In-search ads behave a little bit differently from other videos on YouTube and from other adverts. This is because clicking on one of them will actually take the user to your YouTube channel where the video will play automatically. You *can't* then link this to your landing page unfortunately, so it's less suitable for making direct sales but much more suitable for creating a large number of subscribers and helping to build trust and authority with your brand. This is your chance to demonstrate the kind of value and information that you're able to deliver and to show off all the other videos that you have on your channel.

You can alternatively set these videos to show simply as regular videos, in which case your visitor will just watch them as they would any other video. They'll be able to see more videos from you and your channel name (next to the 'ad' label) in the top right of the screen.

MORE

When you create in-search video ads, there are a few more things to consider as well. For one, your advert can also appear in the sidebar of other videos and as 'suggested' videos. When someone clicks on your advert here, it will play just as any other video would and this is another opportunity for you to get more exposure.

Likewise, your videos can *also* appear over the top of video home pages. So if a user logs in and sees their recommended videos, your ad may appear above that in a similar manner to an in-search ad and they might then choose to visit it.

Another option to consider is that you can add captions and annotations to your videos, which can be a better way to link to external pages. This is actually a way you can circumvent the limitations of in-search ads as you can use these captions to link directly to landing pages or your website.

Of course this means that you can also blur the lines between your regular videos and your adverts. For instance, you could use an in-search video ad that takes visitors to your channel and from there they might watch your video and then see some of your *other* videos which include captions and annotations linking to your landing pages or ecommerce stores.

CHAPTER 5

ADVANCED TECHNIQUES

At this point, you may now be ready to pull your hair out. We've covered an *awful lot* and we still haven't finished explaining the ins-and-outs of your video ad campaign or all of the various different options. You have to think about AdWords, YouTube, account settings, advert types, destinations, bidding and much more – all of which is getting pretty complicated.

And now we're going to hit you with the advanced techniques which range from more advanced targeting, to thumbnail creation and ideal video length. That's before we've even touched on the best practices for making stunning videos with high production values.

Don't let all this scare you. It sounds like an awful lot but once you get stuck in and try it for yourself, you should find that it's actually surprisingly self-explanatory. The first and main tip then to begin with is just to dive in and start playing around with the different features – you know enough now to do that. Set a low budget and experiment with driving some traffic to your brand.

Once you've done that, make yourself a strong cup of coffee and head back here for some more advanced techniques you can use to squeeze a bit more profit and performance out of your ad campaign.

CHOOSING A LENGTH FOR YOUR VIDEO

When creating your video ad, one of the most important factors to consider is how long you want to make it.

The general consensus here is that shorter tends to be better. Remember that you pay for a full view if your visitors last over 30 seconds, so there's no benefit in trying to make your videos tiresomely long. Getting viewers to watch to the end of your video will give you the best chance of engaging and of making an impression that leads to a sale and statistics *regularly* show that shorter videos stand the best chance of being watched through to the end.

Another consideration is that longer videos tend to cost you more. Now this might come as something of a surprise seeing as your views are supposed to be calculated via bidding but it all has to do with a new feature: Google's 'quality measure'.

You see, Google doesn't want advertisers to be able to ruin its search engine or video service by creating spammy videos that are poorly made and promote low quality products but they also don't have time to manually vet every advert that gets uploaded.

As such, the best strategy that Google has for ensuring *some* level of quality is to use an algorithm that attempts to gauge how good the content on your page is. To do this, it uses something called a 'quality measure' which awards better quality content. That means you'll be rewarded with more views and lower CPV if your videos get watched all the way through and you'll *also* be rewarded for shorter videos.

There's nowhere in the official documentation where this is explicitly stated, however many prominent digital marketers have run experiments to test how much YouTube ads cost at different lengths and the results have repeatedly demonstrated that *longer videos cost more*.

Then again, there are still some arguments in favor of longer videos. One is that longer videos might still prevent people from watching to the 30 second mark and thus get you some free brand awareness (this is a key point to bear in mind – even if someone skips your video, you can still show off your branding, so put it right at the start!). Think about it – if an ad starts playing and you notice that it is 20 minutes long, then you may be more inclined to hit skip even if you otherwise would have given it a chance. If your objective is to gain a little brand visibility and you're not bothered about direct conversions, then this can be a smart and effective strategy.

Another consideration is that you can use a longer video to quickly develop more trust and engagement and to demonstrate real value. In other words, rather than relying on the viewer finding your page and looking through your content, you can hit them right away with a big, definitive video explaining a topic or providing stellar entertainment that wouldn't fit into a shorter video.

Again, some of this will come down to experimentation and tweaking. Try different lengths and look at your metrics to see which videos are getting watched all the way through, which are generating clicks and which are generally offering the very best ROI.

LINKING TO YOUR WEBSITE

As mentioned, it is possible to link in-search ads to any page on your website such as a landing page or a link by using captions. You can also do this with the other videos on your channel and this is a great way to drive more traffic to your sales pages and to increase profits. It also makes a lot of sense from a long-term content marketing perspective. In other words, you can use video ads to promote your channel and gain subscriptions, then encourage people to buy from you in your regular videos after they've had a chance to familiarize themselves with your brand and the kind of value you're capable of delivering on a consistent basis.

To do this though, you need to first associate your website with your YouTube account. Before you do this, you won't be able to link to it – and this means you also can't link to other sites (such as using direct affiliate links).

To link your YouTube account to your website, you need to first verify your account, which you can do by going to youtube.com/verify.

You also need to ensure that your account is in good standing – that means that you mustn't have breached any of YouTube's terms and conditions, which relates in particular to the use of copyright footage and audio.

Now you need to go to 'Advanced Channel Settings', which can be found under Creator > Studio > Channel > Advanced (unfortunately, nothing is particularly intuitive with Google and it takes a lot of digging around to find the things you need).

Now look for the 'associated website' section and enter your URL. It will now say 'pending'. Under the URL box, click 'verify' and you'll then be taken to the search console. Here, you need to make sure you're logged in with the same Google Account and you'll need to follow the further instructions to add your site to the search console. You'll then be asked to choose a verification method, which in most cases will simply mean adding a snippet of code to your pages that Google can subsequently detect. Once the verification is complete, the status will go from pending to success and you can then use an annotation to take your visitors anywhere on your URL.

Note: When a viewer clicks on your annotation, playback will stop and this will impact on your watch-time metrics.

Note 2: If you *do* want to link to another destination, then you can always put the link in your video description which will appear underneath the video. This then means that you could in theory link straight to an affiliate product and you can even mention in the video that the link is 'down below' to draw attention to it. There are *tons* of options here.

ADVANCED TARGETING
USER INTERESTS

Another way of targeting is to target a particular user interest which is a relatively new option from Google. This lets you target *people* rather than videos – for instance, you might choose to look for people who watch lots sports videos, who stay up-to-date with the news, or who like videos on technology.

In many ways, this option is actually *better* than targeting the topics of videos. That's because targeting user interests allows you to look more at the long term patterns and behaviors of visitors in order to get a better idea of who they are and even perhaps some of their statistics.

Look at it this way: you have probably watched Taylor Swift videos on YouTube at *some point* in your life, even though you might not be the biggest Taylor Swift fan. If you were shown adverts for the new Britney album at that time, then those ads will have been wasted. It may even have been at a party, in which case no one would have seen the adverts.

On the other hand though, if you are someone who *always* watches video reviews for smartphones, then even when you watch a Taylor Swift video as a one-off, you might *still* be shown the advert for the new iPhone. This makes much more sense in the majority of cases and means that the ads will often be even more highly targeted.

You can even get tricky and try considering how user interests might reflect demographic. For instance, if you were a brand selling a car, then you might choose to look for viewers who look at travel videos. Why? Because travel videos suggest that the viewer has a bigger disposable income and thus may be more likely to afford a 'big ticket' item like a car. Conversely, you might look for someone who looks at style websites and show them videos on dating – again there could be some crossover in the demographics here.

TARGETING SPECIFIC VIDEOS

Did you know that you can also target a *specific* YouTube video? If you have found content created by another user that you think is absolutely perfectly related to your subject matter, then you could use their video as a springboard to support your brand and your campaign.

All you have to do is to paste the URL of that video into the 'placement target' field.

The only risk here is that a single video will of course have significantly less traffic than multiple different videos spread out across an entire subject matter. Again though, this all depends on your strategy. If you want to be as targeted as possible and to really convert a very specific niche then you can find a video that's being watched *only* by the kind of person who might be interested in buying your products.

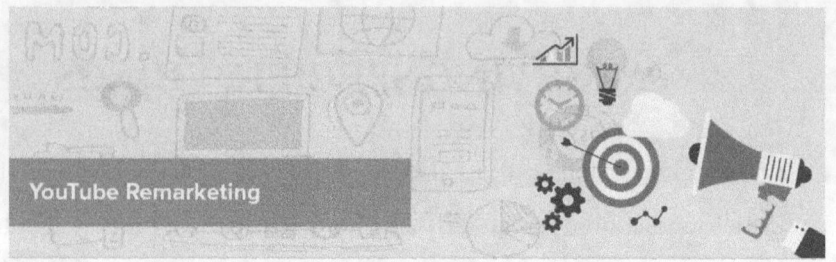

YOUTUBE REMARKETING

Google remarketing is another advanced targeting technique which can be used with YouTube.

Basically, remarketing means that you are showing adverts to people who have already shown an interest in your content. This works by storing cookies on their computers which YouTube can later use to identify them unless they clear the cookies out of their system and by looking at the user accounts of those users.

This is great because it allows you to once again avoid people who have no interest in your content and the options available here are also quite varied allowing you to pick very specific people to advertise to. The options here include:

- Users who have watched any of your videos before
- Users who have taken an action such as clicking 'like' or leaving a comment
- People who have previously viewed your videos in an in-stream ad

- People who have subscribed to your channel

All these options are great and again they vary in terms of their scope and how targeted they are. Going only for people who have liked or commented will significantly limit the number of people your ads are exposed to but these are key and critical people because they have shown a willingness to engage with your content, to actual *listen* to what you're saying and to follow links. It shows much more engagement and trust if someone actually interacts with your brand, versus simply watching your video – which may even have been a mistake.

Obviously there's also nothing to stop you from using multiple different marketing strategies at once to reach a broad but highly targeted audience. For example, you could opt to use remarketing for people who have liked your content, to put your ads on some specific videos and to advertise to people with specific interests.

THUMBNAIL

Your thumbnail is another highly crucial element of your campaigns and especially when it comes to in-search ads. Your thumbnail is essentially the small image that will show when your video appears in search results or suggested videos. This is also important for your general YouTube marketing strategy and for all the other videos on your account.

The aim of your thumbnail is to grab attention and to stand out among other videos. At the same time though, it should ideally match your *other* videos so that you have a consistent 'feel' across your whole channel. This means that you might use the same font on all your thumbnails for instance.

Either way, the ideal thumbnail image is going to be 1280x720 (make sure to at least use this ratio so that no part of your image is cropped) and should be designed to be as eye-catching and clickable as possible. Of course some things we find more eye catching and more clickable than others. People for instance catch our eye easily and especially if they look happy, successful or attractive. If your channel relates to fitness or bodybuilding, then a thumbnail featuring a guy in amazing shape might be appropriate and the more outlandish the physique, the more this will stand out.

CHAPTER 6

CREATING STUNNING YOUTUBE VIDEO ADS

Of course though, in order for your YouTube advertising campaign to be a success, you need to ensure that you have high quality videos comprising your channel and the adverts themselves. No matter how clever you are with your advanced optimization, your bidding strategy or your targeting, your videos need to be high quality if you're going to get people to actually watch them and maybe buy your products.

This is the part that can end up scaring off a lot of potential marketers – but as we'll see it's perfectly possible to create great videos without needing the help of Steven Spielberg. In fact, if you're concerned about creating videos that feature you in front of the camera, you can actually still be successful without having to even *own* a camera. But we'll get to that option in a bit...

THE CONVENTIONAL METHOD: CREATING VIDEOS WITH A CAMERA

Most people *are* going to want to create their own YouTube videos and this is going to mean going in front of the camera. So how do you go about this?

HARDWARE

The first step is of course to invest in a decent camera if you can. Thankfully, most cameras these days will record in at least 1080p and you shouldn't have to spend too much to get a camera that does this. Some other features worth looking into though include wide angle lenses (which will enable you to include more inside the image) and the option to add a microphone for better audio. This latter feature is particularly important if your room has poor acoustics and your videos otherwise come out echoing or quiet.

Note as well, that a lot of displays these days are actually higher than 1080p and this is only going to be a trend that continues. If you want to future proof your tech and your videos themselves, then it might be worth investing in a 2K or even 4K camera.

Now you're looking at spending a fair amount of money though, which is why a good strategy for many marketers is actually to use a camera phone. Believe it or not, many camera phones actually rival dedicated camcorders these days. The excellent camera on the Galaxy S6 and Note5 phones for instance are actually capable of recording 4K *and* they have excellent video stabilization and other features.

Seeing as you also get a phone when you buy one of these cameras *and* you can get it on a monthly contract with no upfront expense, this is a great way to save money and to manage your cash flow as a solo entrepreneur.

VIDEO EDITING SOFTWARE

That's your hardware sorted out but from there you also need to get some good software. In this case, that means a video editing suit such as Adobe Premier or Sony Vegas. Now unfortunately, neither of these are cheap which is why some people will choose to use the free Windows Movie Maker instead. Movie Maker is severely lacking in terms of what it's capable of though and so it's going to be worth the added investment for most people to get the right software.

Fortunately, you can try Adobe Premier for one month free before you have to pay and there are also significant student discounts if you happen to know someone willing to share their student email address with you!

Good video editing software will let you add things like attractive transitions, video overlays, effects and more and there are a few things you can use here to really improve the look and feel of your videos.

EDITING

When editing your videos, the key is to record yourself speaking for longer takes but then to cut rapidly. Give yourself lots of footage to work with but then don't *linger* on shots – you want to keep a consistent momentum.

Add your logo to the video to make it look more professional and to give it more of a professional feel and cut between shots of your speaking and other footage with your voice narrating it. Videos that consist of a single person speaking in their bedroom will generally just look low quality and possibly even embarrassing…

Adding music in the background can help you to give your video a more professional feel and at the same time to ramp up the emotion just how you want it to encourage a sale. Make sure when you do this, that you don't drown out your own voice and that you don't use music that you don't own the rights to. If you don't have any music to hand then one option is to consider using a site like Fiverr to commission someone to write you a score. Otherwise, you can use music from a band if you know anyone musical, or you can use music that's 'royalty free' which means you can use it without paying.

Either way, making sure that your music isn't copyright will help you to avoid getting into trouble and avoiding free music available through YouTube will prevent you from looking unprofessional.

SET-UP

If you're going to be featuring in your video then of course it is important that you look the part. This doesn't mean that you have to be a super model, but if you want to inspire trust then you need to speak confidently and fluently and you need to be well dressed. If you don't come across on the screen as a charismatic presence then *find someone who does*. You can hone your presentation skills as well by filming yourself and watching it back and a general tip is to try speaking more slowly to avoid sounding nervous or stumbling over your words.

Also important is the correct lighting and ideal here is what is known as 'Rembrandt lighting' where you light your face from the side in order to create some contrasting shadows. You should also look into setting up your backdrop to look professional and you should choose somewhere with good acoustics unless you're using a mic.

CHAPTER 7

THE SALES VIDEO

While the previous explanation showed you how to create a more traditional video where you put yourself in front of the camera and then either 'vlog' or sell your product directly, you'll find that many digital marketers actually don't use this strategy at all. Instead, a lot of video marketing is based around videos that follow a simple script to outline the benefits of the product.

These can be *highly* effective and they don't necessarily require you to go in front of a camera at all – or even own one!

CREATING VIDEOS WITHOUT A CAMERA

But if all that sounds like hard work, you *can* make videos without a camera.

One option here is to create a slideshow in PowerPoint and it's actually possible to simply save this as a video file. All you need to do is record your voice narrating the video – or to add in the voice of someone else (you can find people who do voiceovers once again on Fiverr).

Another option is to create an animation. This could be a whiteboard animation, a cartoon or even a stop-motion animation. Again, these can all be created yourself, using specialist software, or by outsourcing to a professional.

MAKING YOUR ADVERTS PERSUASIVE

Either way, what's most important is that your video is effective at grabbing attention, at holding attention and at persuading viewers to click through to your website, to subscribe to your channel or to buy your product.

There are several things you can do to accomplish this but most important is the script and storyboard. The first thing your video has to do is to shock the user and intrigue them so that they want to keep watching. If your advert is more traditionally aimed at selling a physical product like a TV ad, then you might do this with a narrative – we love stories and find it hard to look away. This story should capture the 'value proposition' of your product, showing how it improves the lives of your users and conveying what it *feels* like to use it. Do this in an efficient and entertaining manner with the right music and a strong call to action at the end and you have the makings of a great ad.

On the other hand, you can use a more modern 'digital marketing' approach which works like a script that gradually introduces the product, shows what it can do for the viewer and then encourages them to buy quickly. Again, this can start with a narrative structure ('I once struggled terribly with money/weight loss') or you can start by outlining a specific problem that the viewer can relate to ('Are you tired of going on diets that never seem to lead anywhere?').

Either way, your main goal is to introduce a problem and then to show the solution – your product. Meanwhile, you need to demonstrate the value proposition of your product and hopefully find a way to make it resonate emotionally with the viewer.

At the same time, you need to fully explain what your product is and this can follow a structure known as 'AIDA': Awareness, Interest, Desire, Action.

To really push that last part – the crucial 'action' element – you need to ensure that you create urgency which can mean alluding to scarcity ('buy now while stocks last!').

CONCLUSION:

Snapchat is one of the most interesting social platforms that is come around in a long time. The way that it allows users to communicate only through pictures and video is very interesting and it will be fascinating to see how the platform develops in the future. Marketing on Snapchat is something that people are starting to do more and more and companies are spending a significant portion of their marketing budget on speaking to those people who use Snapchat.

In this book, we've gone over some of the reasons that you should use this social media platform and even took you through the entire sign up process so you can get your account online. We also showed you how to create your QR code which you will be able to use on all kinds of things like your website, the wall of your brick-and-mortar business, other places you decide to put it like your business cards and even other social media platforms.

Some of the highlights of the other areas that were discussed in the book include: taking you through the process of building stories and showing you how you can get fans by using the stories as well as how you can get your initial following. There was also a great deal of information on using analytics and how you can use the numbers for Snapchat gives you to measure your own success. You can also use the analytics companies that are out there that promise to give you detailed information about your marketing efforts. Finally, we went over several ways that you can use Snapchat with other social media platforms and things like live events as well as give you some ideas on how to get followers – like using rand influencers.

It is our hope that the information in this book will allow you to start using Snapchat and be able to use all of the features successfully without any problems. While there is no guarantee that a marketing campaign on Snapchat will be successful, there must be a reason why so many companies are starting to use Snapchat to do marketing. Since other people have found a great deal of success and companies are spending three quarters of a million dollars a day just to be listed on the platform, odds are good that you will find success as well.

And there you have it: everything you need to know to start creating a highly effective YouTube video advertising campaign. It's a lot to take in but once you get stuck in, you'll find that it's easy and actually quite fun to learn on the job.

So where you do you go from here? After creating your account, the best thing to do is to try creating a simple video that sells a product by using people on Fiverr to create a whiteboard animation, or by making something in Excel. You can then set this up as a simple In-Stream advert and link it to a sales page selling your own information product or an affiliate product. This will very quickly teach you the basics of YouTube advertising and you'll be able to learn what works and how to get set up.

From here, you can then go about building your YouTube channel by adding more content, setting up your page and trying out different advanced targeting options etc.

Over time, you'll find that you grow and you're able to increase traffic to your channel and drive more conversions and profit.

And as you do, keep in mind these tips to help you get even more from your efforts:

Consistent Branding

Keep your branding consistent across your videos and across your social media and website. Key to this is creating a great logo and again, it's worth commissioning someone to do this if you're unsure of your own skills in that department!

Make Your Videos Discoverable

You can set your adverts to be unlisted to prevent them showing up in searches but it's not really the best move. It makes much more sense to let people discover your content and that way you can be seen by even more people!

Watch Your Metrics!

Keeping an eye on your metrics is the number one way to see what's working and what's not. Watch your analytics closely and tweak your videos and targeting for the best possible outcome.

Match Your Strategy to Your Brand

Don't create a brand and then try to market it – create a product with a vision for how you'll market it right at the start. This means researching niches, thinking about your current contacts and generally coming up with a synergistic plan.

And Your Video to Your Strategy

Likewise, make sure that your video is right for its intended purpose. Decide which type of YouTube ad you'll be making *before* you create the video. This is important as you'll need your video to be the right length for it to be selectable for certain types of advertising campaign.

Watch the Competition

Watching the competition closely is a great way to get an idea for what works and for the rhythm of good video ads.

Build Your Channel

Don't think of your YouTube ads and your channel as separate entities

– build them up together at the same time and one will support the other. Apart from anything else, having only 100 subscribers somewhat undermines your point when you're talking about your amazing internet marketing skills!

There are many, many more tips and trips of course but you'll learn these as you go. Time to dive in and make a start on your journey to YouTube advertising excellence!

NEXT STEPS

Thank you reading this book. We hope that you found it useful and that it has given you the information you need to help you better understand the importance of managing your online reputation and the strategies to employ to help you do just that.

If you would like additional assistance, please contact us at:

Info@MtJuliet1.com

www.MtJuliet1.com and **www.NewzPosts.com**

www.ingramcontent.com/pod-product-compliance
Lightning Source LLC
Chambersburg PA
CBHW071441180526

170CB00001B/405